Hearsays on Charity Street

Ant Lyubov

BookLeaf Publishing

India | USA | UK

Presentation by *BookLeaf Publishing*

Web: www.bookleafpub.com

E-mail: info@bookleafpub.com

ISBN : 9789357447546

First edition 2021

DEDICATION

For the ones who are ever so tender to listen.

ACKNOWLEDGEMENT

To our Creator who has made us a new wine
Humbly, I thank Thee for the gift of rhyme.

PREFACE

There was once a street named Charity
A long stretch it was, life there is busy
People knew people by face if not by name
A few who lived there, not one is the same.

Been walking on this street since I learned
about life
It's bitter, it's sweet, it's sour deep inside
Each step, every pavement, each tree
giving shade
Paint a picture each day differently. The kind of
hues which never fade

An ongoing battle between truth and falsehood
The murmurs keep ringing waking all
in the hood
The whispers and hearsays are spreading like a
flu
If you dare to read on, it will pass on to you.

grateful

Grateful of things that I have, and I don't
Grateful of things that come and go
Grateful of the peachy, rosy, pinkish sky
Grateful of my unanswered when and why.

TOTO

20 Charity Street

There was once a boy named Toto
His family a bunch of ten
He sells trinkets by day
    and plays with friends at night
He said, "Someday, I'll be a ship captain".

One humid Friday night,
It was then the start of summer
Toto and friends while playing on the street
Was hit by a drunk truck driver.

Some say Toto has instantly died.
Some say the boy was still alive.
The bunch of nine gathered around
Silently, where Toto lies.

LUCY

3 Charity Street

On a lighter note,
   meet the street's newscaster, Lucy
She's short and sweet,
   yet the street's source of truth
She knows every household story,
   every spoken word
And every detail of the latest scoop.

One busy Saturday morning
While Lucy was on her element
Her husband brought home a lady
And left Lucy in shocking torment.

Some say not a word she's spoken for a week
Been waiting for her to spill the tea
But a whisper Lucy heard one evening,
"Pick yourself up, you've got to get going.
   Your man, well, let him be".

the joy of being a mother

A child's hug and warm kisses
The joy of being a mother
The smile they put on their faces
Like there is no other.

Messy kitchen and the waiting dishes are gritty
The laundry that is taking her forever
Toys on the floor, walls of graffiti
Can she still find joy out of this clutter?

Greyish hair and deep-set eyes
Few pounds around, few clothes to fit her
At daytime, forgetfulness her alibis
At nighttime, her thoughts won't leave her.

OLD MAN

1 Charity Street

In the biggest house on Charity Street,
   lived an old man as old as his tales
With wrinkly skin and almost blind set of eyes,
   he smiled to every passerby
Rarely he got visits, the "forgotten one" they say
You'll never get tired of his stories of war,
   yet no one knows his name.

One bright sunny noon,
   while sipping coffee at his porch
When he decided to take a nap,
   Thus his coffee ran cold.
As night falls, there came passersby noticing
   the old man is still
One came close, as he reached out,
   the old man's coffee spilled.

A great relief from the passerby's face,
   the old man is not (yet) dead
"Countless souls that man outlived",
   "Must be black magic!", they said.
Out of all these chatters and noises,
   a whisper the old man heard
"It's not yet time, but you'll know when.
   Get in, you might catch a cold".

AGA

15 Charity Street

I've never known anyone as happy
   as this man named Aga
Each night his friends come over,
   they laugh so hard I shiver
He got the looks, but he sweats so much even
   in cold December nights
At times, alone. At times, he'll find himself
   in a fight.

One Monday afternoon,
   his friends came by so early
They strung the guitar, raised their glasses,
   they laughed, they shouted so loudly
Then came the night, the sky is clear,
   the stars are ever so bright
But in Aga's room,
   so queer to hear the silence pale as white.

Hell breaks loose, he's resisting confinement
A few say, he is mentally ill
The much-needed whisper
   calmed Aga so sudden
Saying, "Child, let yourself be healed".

man of doubt

There was once a man of doubt,
   he didn't try a thing
One day, Courage visited and
     showed him what it brings
"Jump! Let go! I am Courage.
    I will catch you from here".
But as a man of doubt, he looked more
    frightened and so, did not adhere.

There was once a man of doubt,
   he didn't try a thing
One day, Luck visited and
   showed him what it brings
"Dare. Be bold. I got your back. I'm Luck".
But as a man of doubt,
   He instead took one step back.

There was once a man of doubt,
   he didn't try a thing
One day, Fate visited and
   showed him what it brings
"Come. You'll not regret it.
   I'll take you where you should be".
But as a man of doubt, he responded,
   "Isn't here where I'm destined to be?"

JEAN

28 Charity Street

And who can forget my neighbor named Jean
She's born a giver
    though she barely makes a living
She gives out food, for sure it's good
She barely smiles, where is the joy in giving?

A month ago, when circus is in town,
    it's carnival delight
That's when I saw Jean's hand slide in
    someone's coat. Yes, in broad daylight.
She saw me, (I) saw her, so she took me for a
    ride. We surely had so much fun.
But when the sky sparkled, in the blink of
    an eye, Jean's nowhere to be found.

Lots of things which are kind of bizarre
    the cops had found in Jean's place
IDs and wallets, all not hers.
    No furniture and no trace.
Gone are the days when Jean would sneak in
    food by my door
Gone is Jean and so her smile, perhaps she's
    given it away before.

SELAH

24 Charity Street

On the topmost floor of an apartment complex
Staring blankly, spacing out to nowhere
Writing on every word, scene, and context -
is Selah in her favorite outfit, sleepwear.

On rainy days, she is by her huge window
Munching on cookies, soda, waiting for an inspo
On sunny days, she's all over the place
Always watching and observing our ways.

I have read some of her pieces,
    they are not that bad
Sadly, some say, big C has gotten her bald
Rocking in her PJs
    while holding her favorite pen
Saying, "Still had reason to live.
    Still got something to pen."

rays of sunshine

Warm sunshine, cold breeze
Green pigments, auburn leaves
Dried sticks, amber skies
A day before comes with a price.

Why are sparrows so full of sorrow?
Thick feathers, inside's hollow
Sinking hues, springing life
And yet tomorrow has been denied.

Bricks and chips burning red
Dust and rocks, cloud's a bed
Blinding pieces fall to ground
Today, the heart pounds a sound.

If the springtime lays its flowers
And if we won't forbid to summer
Shall the sun set at day?
Shall scarlet paint my ray?

JACQUELIN

4 Charity Street

This girl from the hood named Jacquelin,
   whom we just can't get enough of
Looking and smelling like roses
   even when the going gets tough
Killer smile, perfect body, glamour,
   beauty, and charm
Deep inside you know she's bad news
   but you'll still choose her in your arms.

I have heard this story about Jacquelin
   not so long ago
One Tuesday evening,
   when she's working late or so -
A decent young man from her office
   caught eyes with her
They've been exchanging glances, smiles,
   and soon enough lovers.

Cute, isn't it? What a stare can do
Some bet and they hope
   it will brew into something true
But Jacquelin lost interest, poor man,
   oh, isn't life so rude?
"Leading on just to end it, Jacquelin,
   will do you no good".

YOUNG LOVERS

22 Charity Street

Two young lovers, so full of life, and so in love
Thrills and romances gushing all odds
One makes melody as sweet as the birds
The other is daydreaming, playing with words.

While they were asleep, the two made a pact
Sealed with love's kiss, honor, and blood
But from a deep sleep, the first has awaken
The other was left in a nightmare's cursing.

Some said, "A moment in time when
    they were not so young
Their eyes met the sky and sang their last song
The pact's been broken long ago, it's been done
Yet the melody hums for the things
    that are gone."

some things

I picked a flower so dainty and white
I get so giddy, it's a wonderful sight
But its petals flew when the wind has blown
There are just some things better left alone.

I shouted aloud from the mountain top
Down to the valley it echoed back
It was heard like a whisper, a murmur I'm afraid
There are just some things better left unsaid.

I prayed for a wish to the heaven's gate
Before I sleep and when I'm awake
My wish was granted but the outcome's none
There are just some things better left undone.

VINCENT

12 Charity Street

Back on the radar, one daredevil I know
Vincent on the block, his lifestyle's never low
All day throwing chips, party, vices, and booze
Spending and cashing
    like there is nothing to lose.

One Wednesday night,
    he's looking dapper than ever
Counting his cash,
    fancy wheels with a chauffeur
Vincent rolled the dice even
    chance's fine as hair
When you've been wanting luck so badly,
    That's when it is rare.

Some say this star has lost its shine that night
Still in thirst of the milk once tasted.
    Now what it's like?
People seen him to this day
    still quenching his crave
"Oh, my dear Vincent,
    your frown's deeper than your grave".

FLINT

6 Charity Street

The next house belongs to a man named Flint
A plenty in his brain though his body a skimp
Not a question he cannot answer,
    not a puzzle he cannot solve
Yet pinch him, how delicate, he cries like a wolf.

One Thursday morning, a hermit came by
With him a riddle not one's ever tried
The news reach Flint, the riddle he has heard
But left him all puzzled, it's out of this world.

Some say, "Flint has gone in search of a clue.
Not one thing he read has led to breakthrough".
The load he has carried is bigger than his size
He's forgotten what he's after, yeah,
    It comes with a price.

DIEGO

16 Charity Street

On the busiest part of Charity Street is
    where Diego's house stands
Pretty decent from the outside yet
    inside are loads of guns
Some say, "His armory can turn
    the street into dust".
So, to Diego, they're all mellow,
    their mouths and eyes - a hush.

One Thursday midnight, Diego hosted a huddle
They went underground for a little buy and sell
But a prankster killed the lights,
    Diego's brain instantly flicked
A bloodbath! Upon lights on,
    The scene's not for the weak.

Some say, they thought it was just
    a distant firework
Most stay mum,
    believing Diego's out in the lurk
What happens underneath seems
    destined not to surface
Deep down lies peacefully
    in a death bed of roses.

the worried warrior

A lot on my list, not a thing has been ticked
Imagining the labor gets me tired,
   makes me sick
Drowning thoughts from yesterday and
   for tomorrow's whatnot
My worries get the best of me,
   My worries they're a lot!

Tomorrow, I will stand in front of a crowd
But now my knees are shaking,
   my heart beats so loud
Drowning thoughts from yesterday and
   for tomorrow's whatnot
My worries get the best of me,
   My worries they're a lot!

I'm trapped with planning,
   don't know if I can achieve
I think I'll not make it; it is so hard to believe
Drowning thoughts from yesterday and
   for tomorrow's whatnot
My worries get the best of me,
   My worries they're a lot!

I am but a soul,
I am but unripe

Wishing I could tell more and
   grace you with these tales
But the ships in a hurry, it's time to set the sails
Look yonder the horizon,
   there is more to this after life
For I am but a soul, I am but unripe.

It's hard to bid goodbye to your first waking day
I held the old man's hand, we are on our way
Look yonder the horizon,
   there is more to this after life
For I am but a soul, I am but unripe.

Wishing I could do more for my fellows dear
All I can but wish, if only they could hear
Look yonder the horizon,
   there is more to this after life
For I am but a soul, I am but unripe.